THE POWER OF

How to Walk ir

the Power of t

CW00496414

THE
POWER OF
THE SACRIFICE

HOW TO WALK IN
VICTORY THROUGH
THE POWER OF THE
BLOOD OF JESUS

DEREK PRINCE

Contents

The Power of the Sacrifice

How do you handle adversity? How do you deal with pressure? Throughout the ages, the human race has displayed a wide range of capabilities when coping with opposition and disappointment – depression, rage, denial or fear. These reactions are even common to people who have a relationship with God.

In my study of the Scriptures, though, I have come to believe that this need not be the case. There must be a way to gain victory over the struggles that we face in life. Surely Christ's suffering, crucifixion and resurrection did more than just rescue us from eternity in hell. The work of the cross has got to have some influence over the way we navigate our circumstances during our time here on earth. I believe it does.

I believe the Bible teaches – and personal experience proves – that the blood of Jesus provides so much more than a ticket to heaven. I believe that when the conditions are met, Christians can apply the blood of Jesus to every area of life – and witness its full effects.

A REVELATION FROM HEAVEN

By way of introduction I am going to begin at the end – the end of the Bible, that is. Revelation speaks about a great end-time conflict that lies ahead at the close of the present age – a conflict in which heaven and earth are involved. The angels of God are involved. Satan and his angels are involved. And God's believing people on earth are involved. Thank God the Bible promises that the victory goes to God and to His people. It describes how the people of God on earth play their part in obtaining that victory. It is a statement made by the angels, but it is made about the believers on earth:

> *They overcame him by the blood of the Lamb and by the word of their testimony, and they did not love their lives to the death.*

Revelation 12:11

The word *they* refers to people like you and me – believers in Jesus Christ. The *him* is Satan. That shows clearly that there can be direct conflict between us and Satan. There is no one else in between: they overcame him.

Then it tells us how they overcame him: *By the blood of the Lamb and by the word of their testimony.* It also adds what kind of people they were: committed – totally committed. That is the only kind of Christian that frightens Satan: a totally committed Christian.

When the Bible says, *They did not love their lives to the death*, it means that, for them, staying alive was not priority number one. Priority number one was to do the will of God, whether they stayed alive or not. The most important thing was to be faithful to the Lord.

THE LORD'S ARMY

We talk about being soldiers in the Lord's army, but I think a lot of us really have a very vague and rather sentimental idea about what it is to be a soldier. By no choice of my own, I was a soldier in the British Army in World War II for over five years. And when I was conscripted, I did not get a nice little certificate from the commanding officer saying, "We guarantee that you'll never have to lose your life." No soldier has ever joined an army on the condition that he will not be killed. In fact, in a certain sense, any time a soldier joins an army, one of the prerequisites is affirming the possibility that he or she may be killed.

It is the same in the Lord's army. You have no guarantee that you will not have to lay down your life. The people that Satan fears are those who are not afraid to lay down their lives. After all, life is comparatively brief. It is not going to go on forever. It would be foolish to miss eternal glory for the sake of a few brief years on earth.

I believe it is enlightened self-interest to have this realigned sense of value – this embracing of what is more important. There is a wonderful statement in 1 John:

> The world and its desires pass away, but the man who does the will of God lives forever.
>
> 1 John 2:17, NIV

When you unite your will with the will of God in total commitment, you become unsinkable. You are undefeatable. You are unshakable.

4

Whether you live or whether you die is of secondary importance, but you cannot be defeated.

HOW TO OVERCOME SATAN

Let's consider what it means to overcome Satan by the blood of the Lamb and by the word of our testimony. We overcome Satan when we testify personally to what the Word of God says the blood of Jesus does for us.

As we explore just exactly how to do that, I want to take an example from the Old Testament – from the Passover ceremonies recorded in Exodus 12. In that ceremony God – through the sacrifice of a Passover lamb – provided total protection for all the people of Israel. But they had to do certain things with the lamb and with its blood to insure that protection. God says:

> *Then Moses called for all the elders of Israel and said to them, "Pick out and take lambs for yourselves according to your families, and kill the Passover lamb. And you shall take a bunch of hyssop, dip it in the blood that is in the basin, and strike the lintel and the two doorposts with the blood that is in the basin. And none of you*

shall go out of the door of his house until morning. For the Lord will pass through to strike the Egyptians, and when He sees the blood on the lintel and on the two doorposts, the Lord will pass over the door and not allow the destroyer to come into your houses to strike you."

Exodus 12:21–23

At a certain given moment each father had to choose a lamb of appropriate size for his family. Then they had to sacrifice the lamb and they had to catch its blood in a basin. Its blood was very precious. None of it was to be spilled on the ground. Still, even with the lamb slain and the blood simply in the basin, it did not protect a single person. The fathers were required to transfer the blood from the basin to the doors of their homes and to smear it or sprinkle it on the lintel and on the two side posts, but never on the threshold. No one was ever to walk over the blood.

So, the entire destiny of Israel depended on getting the blood from the basin to the door without any of it touching the ground. How were they to do it? With a weed. Hyssop is a kind of a

6

wild plant that grows everywhere in the Middle East. God instructed them to pluck a little bunch of hyssop, dip it in the blood in the basin and sprinkle the blood over the door with it. I find it interesting that this humble, unimportant weed became essential to the salvation of Israel.

Then God issued one more requirement. He said once the blood had been sprinkled on the doorposts and lintel, the Israelites had to stay inside the house. That is where the protection was. If they were to go outside the blood, they would be unprotected.

Now, let's relate this to us. Paul says, in 1 Corinthians 5:7, Christ (the Lamb) is our Passover who was sacrificed for us (the blood is in the basin). But remember, the blood in the basin does not protect anybody. We are in the same situation as Israel. We have to get the blood from the basin to the place where we live. Then we are protected – provided we are obedient.

So, how do we get the blood of the sacrifice (Jesus) from the basin to the place where we live? This is where Revelation 12:11 becomes crucial: *They overcame him by the blood of the Lamb and by the word of their testimony.*

We overcome Satan when we testify personally to what the Word of God says the blood of Jesus does for us. Our personal attestation of its power is what gets the blood from the basin to where we live. In this context, the word *testimony* is not referring to the whole story of how you became a Christian. It is simply saying a few words according to the Scripture. It is like the little hyssop, but it saves us. It is our protection.

SAYING THE SAME AS GOD'S WORD

I cannot overemphasize the importance of your testimony. Hebrews reinforces this point:

> *Therefore, holy brethren, partakers of the heavenly calling, consider the Apostle and High Priest of our confession, Christ Jesus.*
>
> Hebrews 3:1

The writer of Hebrews calls Jesus the "High Priest of our confession." Confession means literally "saying the same as." For us as believers in the Bible and in Jesus Christ, confession means we say the same with our mouths as God says in His Word. We make the words of our mouth agree with the Word of God.

Jesus is the High Priest of our confession. No confession; no high priest. Without our conscious, intentional agreement with God's Word, Jesus cannot represent you before God. He can only advocate on your behalf when you make the right confession. In Matthew, Jesus said, *"By your words you will be justified, and by your words you will be condemned"* (12:37). You settle your destiny by the words you speak.

James said the tongue is like the rudder on a ship. It is a very small part of the ship, but it determines exactly where the ship will go (James 3:4). And we determine the course of our lives by the way we use our tongues. Many Christians are very careless and delinquent in the way they use their tongues: "I'm dying to see you." "I was tickled to death." "I was so embarrassed, I just wanted to die." Generally, I believe it would be wise to never say anything about yourself that you would not want Jesus to make happen.

And do not sell yourself short, because God holds you in very high regard. He invested the blood of Jesus in you. When you criticize yourself, what you are really doing is criticizing God's handiwork. In Ephesians, Paul says we are His workmanship (Ephesians 2:10). I believe it is dangerously presumptuous to criticize the workmanship of God. Pride, of course, is rampant among Christians, but another problem that is just as great is underestimating yourself.

APPLYING THE BLOOD OF JESUS

The "word of our testimony" is the means of applying the blood of Jesus to the place where we live. But, obviously, you can only testify as to what the Word of God says about the blood of Jesus when you actually know what the Word of God says. So, one essential requirement is knowing what the Bible teaches about the blood of Jesus. There are seven major ways in which the New Testament reveals the blood of Jesus works for us that we will explore in the next chapters.

Redemption

In Ephesians 1:7, Paul says, *"In Him we have redemption through His blood."* Redemption means "being bought back." We were in the hands of the devil, and Jesus bought us back with His blood. Peter explains further:

> *Knowing that you were not redeemed with corruptible things, like silver or gold, from your aimless conduct received by tradition from your fathers, but with the precious blood of Christ, as of a lamb without blemish and without spot.*
>
> 1 Peter 1:18–19

Notice Peter's use of the word lamb, taking us back to the Passover. Jesus was without blemish – without original sin. He was without spot – without personal sin. And we have been redeemed by His blood.

Now let's look at Psalm 107 and see the practical application of this:

> *Let the redeemed of the Lord say so, whom He has redeemed out of the hand of the enemy.*
>
> verse 2

If we are redeemed, we have to say so. No "say so," no redemption. It is your confession – your testimony – that makes it work for you. Otherwise, the blood remains in the basin.

By way of example – and this is not the only way it could be said – you could speak out loud these words:

Through the blood of Jesus, I have been redeemed out of the hand of the devil.

I have no doubt about where I was when Jesus met me. I was in the hand of the devil – there is no question in my mind about that. But I am not there today, because I have been redeemed by the blood of Jesus out of the hand of the devil. When you can get past pride and awkwardness and speak your testimony out loud, you will begin to experience freedom like you have never known.

Cleansing

John identifies the second way the blood of Jesus works for us:

> But if we walk in the light as He is in the light, we have fellowship with one another, and the blood of Jesus Christ His Son cleanses us from all sin.　　　　　1 John 1:7

In the original language all the verbs in that verse are in the continuing present tense. It is important to see that. If we continue walking in the light, we continue to have fellowship with one another. Notice that the evidence of walking in the light is that you have fellowship (relationship, interaction) with other believers.

The natural presumption would be that if you find yourself out of fellowship, you should examine yourself to see if you are continuing to walk in the light.

The blood does not cleanse in the dark. If you get out of the light – if you allow yourself to operate in the shadows – your relationships will suffer and, more importantly, you compromise the power of the blood of Jesus to cleanse you.

This is a continuing provision. It applies no matter where we are, so long as we are in the light.

You may be in the most defiling circumstances, among the most wicked people. There may be countless evil pressures against you. But as long as you are walking in the light, the blood is continually cleansing you from all sin.

Psalm 51 is the great penitent psalm of David. After he had been convicted of his two terrible sins of adultery and murder, he turned to God with his tremendous cry of repentance and plea for mercy. In verse 7 he says, *"Purge me with hyssop, and I shall be clean, wash me, and I shall be whiter than snow."*

Here we see yet another reference to the Passover: hyssop. David was coming out of the shadows to appropriate the cleansing power of God.

What an assurance it is to know where you can go when you are guilty. Stop for a moment and think about the billions of people who are guilty and do not know where to go. Imagine what it would be like to have a guilty conscience – to be tormented with the impact of your sin – and not know where to go to find forgiveness and peace. That is the condition of humanity today.

To make practical application of this truth, you might say, out loud, something like this:

While I walk in the light, the blood of Jesus cleanses me, now and continually, from all sin.

This declares that you are covered not only at this moment, but from this moment on as long as you are walking in the light.

Justification

Justification is one of those theological words that people often do not know how to define. The Greek word in its basic form means "to make righteous," but it has several different shades of meaning. Paul writes:

> *Much more then, having now been justified by His blood, we shall be saved from wrath through Him.* Romans 5:9

Suppose you are on trial in a court of law for a capital offense. Your life is at stake. When the verdict comes out not guilty, that is justification. You have been acquitted.

But justification means more than acquittal. You have been made righteous – in right standing with God – with the righteousness of Jesus Christ. If you relied on your own righteousness, you could not even get close to being in right standing with God. So, you have to rely on the righteousness of Jesus Christ.

I have coined a phrase I use to explain justification: I am justified, just-as-if-I'd never sinned. Why? Because I have been made righteous with the righteousness of Jesus Christ. And He never sinned. He had no guilt. He had no past to be covered up. Isaiah puts it beautifully:

> *I will greatly rejoice in the Lord. My soul shall be joyful in my God; for He has clothed me with the garments of salvation, He has covered me with the robe of righteousness.* Isaiah 61:10

Isaiah is celebrating two provisions: salvation and righteousness. When you trust in Jesus Christ and His sacrifice on your behalf, you will be clothed with a garment of salvation. But it does not stop there. You will be covered with the robe of righteousness. One translation says, *He has "wrapped me [around] with the robe of righteousness"* (NASB).

You are totally covered with the righteousness

of Jesus Christ. The devil has nothing he can say against you. If he reminds you of everything you have done wrong, agree with him. Say, "You're quite right, Satan. But that's all in the past. Now I am clothed with the righteousness of Jesus Christ. See if you can find anything wrong with that!"

Now let's apply this out loud:

Through the blood of Jesus, I am justified, acquitted, not guilty, reckoned righteous, made righteous, just-as-if-I'd never sinned.

Sanctification

We find the next application of the blood of Jesus in Hebrews:

> Therefore Jesus also, that He might sanctify the people with His own blood, suffered outside the gate.
>
> Hebrews 13:12

In the original Greek, the verb to sanctify is directly related to the word for holiness. *Sanct* is the same word we have in English for saint. So "to sanctify" is to make saintly or to make holy. It means "to be set apart."

There are two aspects to this: what we are set apart *from*, and what we are set apart *to*. We are set apart from sin and from everything that defiles. And then we are made holy with God's own holiness.

Talking about God's chastisement, Hebrews says our human fathers chastised us for a short period of our lives according to their best judgment. But God does it in a different way:

> *For they indeed for a few days chastened us as seemed best to them, but He for our profit, **that we may be partakers of His holiness.***
>
> Hebrews 12:10

Notice again that we bring nothing to the table. We are not made holy through our own holiness any more than we are made righteous through our own righteousness. We partake of His holiness through the blood of Jesus. The verbal declaration of that would be something like this:

Through the blood of Jesus I am sanctified, separated from sin, set apart to God, made holy with God's holiness.

$\mathcal{L}ife$

The blood of Jesus does not only save us from sin, it gives us something positive as well – life.

> *"For the life of the flesh is in the blood, and I have given it to you upon the altar to make atonement for your souls."*   Leviticus 17:11

It is the blood that makes atonement for the soul. So the life of God – the life of the Creator – comes to us through the blood of Jesus.

Our human minds have no way to calculate the potential of that statement because the Creator is infinitely greater than all that He has created.

If we could only grasp the totality of the power that is in the blood of Jesus. There is more power in one drop of the blood of Jesus than

P70

there is in the entire kingdom of Satan – because in the blood of Jesus is the eternal, uncreated, measureless life of God Himself, a life that existed before anything was ever created.

With that in mind let's look at John 6:

> Then Jesus said to them, "Most assuredly, I say to you, unless you eat the flesh of the Son of Man and drink His blood, you have no life in you. Whoever eats my flesh and drinks My blood has eternal life, and I will raise him up at the last day. For My flesh is food indeed, and My blood is drink indeed. He who eats My flesh and drinks My blood abides in Me, and I in him. As the living Father sent Me, and I live because of the Father, so he who feeds on Me will live because of Me." John 6:53–57

I began my Christian ministry in 1946 in an Arab town called Ramallah just north of Jerusalem. At that time the language of our home was Arabic. And whenever I think of the communion service, I still always think back to what the Arabs said: "Let us drink the blood of Jesus." That was not some strange, super-spiritual phrase; that was their way of talking about the communion. There may be many ways to apply this, but, for me, when I take communion, I receive the life that is in the blood of Jesus. Some of us have been taught that we do it just as a memorial. That is not what Jesus said. He said, "You're eating My flesh and you're drinking My blood."

There are many different opinions as to how it becomes life to us. The Catholics and the liturgical churches believe it is through consecration by a priest. Frankly, that is not what I believe. I believe it comes through faith. When I receive it in faith believing what Jesus said in His Word, it becomes to me precisely what He said it would be. And it is through this that He imparts life. Paul says:

> Is not the cup of thanksgiving for which we give thanks a participation in the blood of Christ? And is not the bread that we break a participation in the body of Christ?
>
> 1 Corinthians 10:16, NIV

A little further on, Paul reminds us of the way the Lord's Supper was instituted:

For I received from the Lord what I also passed on to you: The Lord Jesus, on the night he was betrayed, took bread, and when he had given thanks, he broke it and said, "This is my body, which is for you; do this in remembrance of me." In the same way, after supper he took the cup, saying, "This cup is the new covenant in my blood; do this, whenever you drink it, in remembrance of me." For whenever you eat this bread and drink this cup, you proclaim the Lord's death until he comes.

1 Corinthians 11:23–26, NIV

It is perfectly true we do this in remembrance of Him, but what do we do in remembrance of Him? We take His body. For me, this is no doctrine or theory; this is a living reality.

My wife Ruth and I used to take communion together as husband and wife every morning. And every morning, I would break the bread and say, "Lord Jesus, we receive this bread as Your flesh." And we would eat it. And then we would share a cup and I would say, "Lord Jesus, we receive this cup as Your blood." Then I would say: "As we do this, we proclaim Your death until You come."

When you have communion, you proclaim the Lord's death until He comes. You are outside of the whole context of immediate time. We have no past but the cross, no future but His coming. We proclaim His death until He comes. And every time we do that, we remind ourselves that He is coming again.

To affirm this verbally you could say:

Lord Jesus, when I receive Your blood, in it I receive Your life, the life of God – divine, eternal, endless life.

Intercession

The last two provisions of the blood take us out of the realm of time and into the heavenly and eternal realms – which is where we want to end up anyway. In Hebrews we find the next application of the blood of Jesus:

> But you have come to Mount Zion, to the heavenly Jerusalem, the city of the living God. You have come to thousands upon thousands of angels in joyful assembly, to the church of the firstborn, whose names are written in heaven. You have come to God, the judge of all men, to the spirits of righteous men made perfect, to Jesus the mediator of a new covenant, and to the sprinkled blood that speaks a better word than the blood of Abel.   Hebrews 12:22–24, NIV

Notice the tense: "You have come." We are not *going* to come, but in the Spirit we *have* come. Eight things are listed to which we have come:

- to Mount Zion;
- to the heavenly Jerusalem (not the earthly Jerusalem, but the heavenly Jerusalem), the city of the living God;
- to an innumerable company of angels;
- to the church of the firstborn who are registered in heaven;
- to God, the Judge of all;
- to the spirits of just men made perfect;
- to Jesus the mediator of the New Covenant;
- and finally, to the blood of sprinkling that speaks better things than that of Abel.

The sprinkled blood of Jesus that speaks on our behalf in heaven is contrasted with the blood of Abel. There are three main points of contrast.

1. Abel's blood was shed against his will. Jesus willingly gave His blood.
2. Abel's blood was sprinkled on earth thou-

sands of years ago. Jesus' blood is sprinkled in the presence of God even at this present time.

3. Abel's blood called out for vengeance, Jesus' blood pleads for mercy.

This is such a beautiful revelation. There are times when we are weak, when we are under pressure. We just can't pray. We just wonder if we are going to be able to draw the next breath. It is good to know at those times that the blood of Jesus – sprinkled in the immediate presence of God – is always speaking on our behalf, calling out for mercy.

Affirm this by saying out loud:

Thank You, Lord, that even when I cannot pray, the blood of Jesus is pleading for me in heaven.

Access to God's Throne

Let's look at Hebrews 10. Notice we begin with boldness. The Greek word means *freedom of speech*. It is very important that our boldness gives us freedom of speech. Remember, the power is in our testimony. If we do not testify, we do not have it.

> *Therefore, brethren, having boldness to enter the Holiest by the blood of Jesus, by a new and living way which He consecrated for us, through the veil, that is, His flesh, and having a High Priest over the house of God, let us draw near with a true heart in full assurance of faith, having our hearts sprinkled from an evil conscience and our bodies washed with pure water. Let us hold fast*

THE POWER OF THE SACRIFICE

the confession of our hope without wavering.

Hebrews 10:19–23

Hebrews 3:1 says Jesus is the *"High Priest of our confession."* Hebrews 4:14 says to *"hold fast your confession."* But Hebrews 10:23 says to hold it fast *"without wavering."* What does that tell you? When you are in an airplane and they say to buckle your seat belts, what do you expect? Turbulence. When the Word of God says to make the confession, hold fast the confession and hold it fast without wavering, that is like God saying to buckle your seat belts, because there will be turbulence. Do not let the turbulence cause you to unbuckle your seat belt. This is when the word of your testimony is most needed – and most effective. Keep on making the right confession. Even when it seems totally contrary to everything around you, God's Word is true.

You will notice that we have access into the Holiest by a new and living way. In Leviticus it tells us that the high priest entered once every year with a censer full of incense that cast a fragrant cloud and covered the Mercy Seat. That is worship. But he also entered with the blood of the sacrifice, and he sprinkled it seven times between the veil and the Mercy Seat. Once, twice, three times, four times, five times, six times, seven times. And then he smeared it on the east side (or the front side) of the Mercy Seat. So, when the writer of Hebrews says we have boldness through the blood of Jesus by a new and living way, he is thinking about that sevenfold sprinkling of the blood and the blood on the Mercy Seat.

We can approach the throne of Almighty God, the holiest place in the universe, with boldness because of the blood of Jesus. We have access – directly to God. And you can affirm it by declaring, out loud:

Thank You, Lord, that through the sprinkled blood of Jesus, I have access into Your presence, into the presence of Almighty God, the holiest place in the universe.

The blood of Jesus – sprinkled seven times – works in us in seven different ways: through redemption, cleansing, justification, sanctification, life, intercession and access. But remember, you overcome Satan by the blood of the Lamb and by the word of your testimony. That is how you enact it in your own life. That is how you apply it. That is what frightens the devil – and gives you ongoing victory.

Your Testimony of Faith

Now that you have come to the end of this study, why not affirm once more all that you have learned about the power of the blood of Jesus by declaring it out loud:

We overcome Satan when we testify personally to what the Word of God says the blood of Jesus does for us:[1]

Through the blood of Jesus, I am redeemed out of the hand of the devil.[2]

Through the blood of Jesus, all my sins are forgiven.[3]

Through the blood of Jesus, I am continually being cleansed from all sin.[4]

Through the blood of Jesus, I am justified, made righteous, just-as-if-I'd never sinned.[5]

Through the blood of Jesus, I am sanctified, made holy, set apart to God.[6]

Through the blood of Jesus, I have boldness to enter into the presence of God.[7]

The blood of Jesus cries out continually to God in heaven on my behalf.[8]

Satan has no place in me, and no power over me, through the blood of Jesus.[9]

References

1 Revelation 12:11– *And they overcame him by the blood of the Lamb* [Jesus Christ]*, and by the word of their testimony, and they did not love their lives to the death.* [That is, they testified to what the Word of God says about the blood of Jesus.]

2 Ephesians 1:7 – *In Him we have redemption through His blood, the forgiveness of sins, according to the riches of His grace.*

2a Psalm 107:2 – *Let the redeemed of the Lord say so, whom He has redeemed from the hand of the enemy.* [ie Let us testify to our redemption.]

3 Ephesians 1:7 – *In Him we have redemption through His blood, the forgiveness of sins, according to the riches of His grace.*

4 1 John 1:7 – *But if we walk in the light as He is in the light, we have fellowship with one another,*

41

and the blood of Jesus Christ His Son cleanses us from all sin.

5 Romans 5:9 – *Much more then, having now been justified by His blood, we shall be saved from wrath through Him.*

6 Hebrews 13:12 – *Therefore Jesus also, that He might sanctify the people with His own blood, suffered outside the gate.*

7 Hebrews 10:19 – *Therefore, brethren, having boldness to enter the Holiest by the blood of Jesus.*

8 Genesis 4:10 – *And He said, "What have you done? The voice of your brother's blood cries out to me from the ground."*

8a Hebrews 12:24 – *To Jesus the Mediator of the new covenant, and to the blood of sprinkling that speaks better things than that of Abel.*

9 1 Corinthians 6:19–20 – *Or do you not know that your body is the temple of the Holy Spirit who is in you, whom you have from God, and you are not your own? For you were bought at a price; therefore glorify God in your body and in your spirit, which are God's.*

About the Author

Derek Prince (1915–2003) was born in India of British parents. He was educated as a scholar of Greek and Latin at Eton College and King's College, Cambridge in England. Upon graduation he held a fellowship (equivalent to a professorship) in Ancient and Modern Philosophy at King's College. Prince also studied Hebrew, Aramaic, and modern languages at Cambridge and the Hebrew University in Jerusalem. As a student, he was a philosopher and self-proclaimed agnostic.

BIBLE TEACHER

While in the British Medical Corps during World War II, Prince began to study the Bible as a philosophical work. Converted through a powerful encounter with Jesus Christ, he was baptized in the Holy Spirit a few days later. Out of this encounter, he formed two conclusions: first, that Jesus Christ is alive; second, that the Bible is a true, relevant, up-to-date book. These conclusions altered the whole course of his life, which he then devoted to studying and teaching the Bible as the Word of God.

Discharged from the army in Jerusalem in 1945, he married Lydia Christensen, founder of a children's home there. Upon their marriage, he immediately became father to Lydia's eight adopted daughters – six Jewish, one Palestinian Arab, and one English. Together, the family saw the rebirth of the state of Israel in 1948. In the late 1950s, they adopted another daughter while Prince was serving as principal of a teacher training college in Kenya. In 1963, the Princes immigrated to the United States and pastored a church in Seattle. In 1973, Prince became one of the founders of Intercessors for America. His book *Shaping History through Prayer and Fasting* has awakened Christians around the world to their responsibility to pray for their governments. Many consider underground translations of the book as instrumental in the fall of communist regimes in the USSR, East Germany, and Czechoslovakia.

Lydia Prince died in 1975, and Prince married Ruth Baker (a single mother to three adopted children) in 1978. He met his second wife, like his first wife, while she was serving the Lord in Jerusalem. Ruth died in December 1998 in Jerusalem, where they had lived since 1981.

TEACHING, PREACHING AND BROADCASTING

Until a few years before his own death in 2003 at the age of eighty-eight, Prince persisted in the ministry God had called him to as he traveled the world, imparting God's revealed truth, praying for the sick and afflicted, and sharing his prophetic insights into world events in the light of Scripture. Internationally recognized as a Bible scholar and spiritual patriarch, Derek Prince established a teaching ministry that spanned six continents and more than sixty years. He is the author of more than fifty books, six hundred audio teachings, and one hundred video teachings, many of which have been translated and published in more than one hundred languages.

He pioneered teaching on such groundbreaking themes as generational curses, the biblical significance of Israel, and demonology. Prince's radio program, which began in 1979, has been translated into more than a dozen languages and continues to touch lives. Derek's main gift of explaining the Bible and its teaching in a clear and simple way has helped build a foundation of faith in millions of lives. His nondenominational, nonsectarian approach has made his teaching equally relevant and helpful to people from all racial and religious backgrounds, and his teaching is estimated to have reached more than half the globe.

DPM WORLDWIDE MINISTRY

In 2002, Derek Prince said, "It is my desire – and I believe the Lord's desire – that this ministry continue the work, which God began through me over sixty years ago, until Jesus returns." Derek Prince Ministries International continues to reach out to believers in over 140 countries with Derek's teaching, fulfilling the mandate to keep on "until Jesus returns." This is accomplished through the outreaches of more than thirty Derek Prince offices around the world, including primary work in Australia, Canada, China, France, Germany, the Netherlands, New Zealand, Norway, Russia, South Africa, Switzerland, the United Kingdom, and the United States. For current information about these and other worldwide locations, visit www.derekprince.com.

INSPIRED BY DEREK'S TEACHING?
HELP MAKE IT AVAILABLE
TO OTHERS!

If you have been inspired and blessed by this Derek Prince resource you can help make it available to a spiritually hungry believer in other countries, such as China, the Middle East, India, Africa or Russia.

Even a small gift from you will ensure that that a pastor, Bible college student or a believer elsewhere in the world receives a free copy of a Derek Prince resource in their own language.

Donate now: www.dpmuk.org/give

BOUGHT WITH BLOOD

At the cross Christ endured all the evil due to you and in turn made available all the good due to Him. In this provocative, Scripture- rich book, acclaimed author Derek Prince explores the nine "divine exchanges" of the atonement.

The study guide at the end of each chapter makes this a perfect book for small group study.

£8.99
ISBN 978-1-908594-91-4
Paperback and eBook

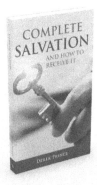

Derek Prince Ministries Offices Worldwide

DPM – Asia/Pacific
38 Hawdon Street
Sydenham
Christchurch 8023
New Zealand: + 64 3 366 4443
E: admin@dpm.co.nz
W: www.dpm.co.nz and www.derekprince.in

DPM – Australia
15 Park Road
Seven Hills
New South Wales 2147
Australia
T: +61 2 9838 7778
E: enquiries@au.derekprince.com
W: www.derekprince.com.au

DPM – Canada
P.O. Box 8354
Halifax
Nova Scotia B3K 5M1
Canada
T: + 1 902 443 9577
E: enquiries.dpm@eastlink.ca
W: www.derekprince.org

DPM – France
B.P. 31, Route d'Oupia
34210 Olonzac
France
T: + 33 468 913872
E: info@derekprince.fr
W: www.derekprince.fr

DPM – Germany
Söldenhofstr. 10
83308 Trostberg
Germany
T: + 49 8621 64146
E: ibl@ibl-dpm.net
W: www.ibl-dpm.net

DPM – Netherlands
Nijverheidsweg 12
7005 BJ Doetinchem
Netherlands
T: +31 251–255044
E: info@derekprince.nl
W: www.derekprince.nl

DPM – Norway
P.O. Box 129
Lodderfjord
N-5881 Bergen
Norway
T: +47 928 39855
E: xpress@dpskandinavia.com
W: www.derekprince.no

Derek Prince Publications Pte. Ltd.
P.O. Box 2046
Robinson Road Post Office
Singapore 904046
T: + 65 6392 1812
E: dpmchina@singnet.com.sg
W: www.dpmchina.org (English)
    www.ygmweb.org (Chinese)

DPM – South Africa
P.O. Box 33367
Glenstantia
0010 Pretoria
South Africa
T: +27 12 348 9537
E: enquiries@derekprince.co.za
W: www.derekprince.co.za

DPM – Switzerland
Alpenblick 8
CH-8934 Knonau
Switzerland
T: + 41 44 768 25 06
E: dpm-ch@ibl-dpm.net
W: www.ibl-dpm.net

DPM – UK
PO Box 393
Hitchin SG5 9EU
United Kingdom
T: + 44 1462 492100
E: enquiries@dpmuk.org
W: www.dpmuk.org

DPM – USA
P.O. Box 19501
Charlotte NC 28219
USA
T: + 1 704 357 3556
E: ContactUs@derekprince.org
W: www.derekprince.org

Lightning Source UK Ltd.
Milton Keynes UK
UKHW022229090421
381737UK00008B/380